*"You Kn_*

"Wonderful! B_
writer tell the nit_ process. This is a straight-to-the-point and to-the-heart approach to deep teachings and truth. Each of her "101 Everyday Indications" is a zinger. Dr. Rosie helps us to embrace the often "not so rosy" journey to authentic awakening."
~ *Joyah French, Transformational Mentor / Teacher*
Creator of Inner Alchemy Half Moon Bay, CA

"In her new book, Rosie Kuhn has cleverly and clearly stated some of the most profound principles of authentic, enlightened, joyful living. You will recognize your own journey on every page and you will find a clear roadmap for reaching your potential. Initially, you will read the book in one sitting because you won't be able to put it down! Later, you can open to any page randomly, as a source of daily inspiration."
~ *Lisa McClenahan, MA, CHT, CLC*
Life & Relationship Coach & Clinical Hypnotherapist
www.mcclenahans.com

"Resonating, deep and thoughtful. This book is a true companion that supports us in daily connection to our essence. I highly recommend it to anyone involved in transformational work. It is beauty and compassion spoken in simple, inspiring words. Enjoy!"
~ *Maria Neizvestnaya. Executive Director, Moscow Training Centre, Moscow, Russia www.mtcentr.ru*

"No matter where you are on the journey, this book will serve you: if you're a beginner, the indicators will inspire you to embark on the road ahead; if you've been transforming and need a boost, they will remind you of how far you've come; and if you've transformed, you will be in awe of how much you've accomplished.
~ *Erin Hinkle, Development Consultant For Nonprofit Organizations, NY, NY.*

YOU KNOW YOU ARE TRANSFORMING WHEN...

101

EVERYDAY INDICATIONS THAT YOU ARE CREATING A LIFE HAPPIER EVER AFTER

BY DR. ROSIE KUHN, PH.D.

© 2013 by Rosie Kuhn, Ph.D.
First published in the United States by The Paradigm Shifts Publishing Co.
PO Box 1637, Eastsound WA 98245
Cover design & formatting by Maureen O'Neill, www.onfirecoaching.com
(Fonts: Adobe Trajan, Trajan Pro and Microsoft Calibri)
Edited by Jessica Rubi Hernandez, www.RubyMoonHealingArts.com

ISBN: 978-0-9835522-8-4

ACKNOWLEDGMENTS

This simple little book, which arrived out of nowhere, in complete form, over a matter of hours, was one of those events that had been gestating for decades; Transformational experiences happen that way. Incremental shifts and changes over years, then one day, plouf!* – it arrives, unceremoniously.

I have been gifted by many incredible teachers, who at the time were masquerading as family members, husbands and children, nature and animals, books and friends. I acknowledge all of you for your contributions to my life as it is, in this moment.

There are only a handful of people who touched this specific work, to whom I owe a huge thank you. Maureen O'Neill, graphic artist extraordinaire, lovingly created the book cover and formatted the entire book. She also assisted in crafting each page so that the words flowed like poetry. I'm so grateful to you Maureen, for your playful, passionate spirit. You are a great companion on this journey of life.

Jessica Ruby Hernandez, Lisa McClenahan, Becca Archer, Erin Hinkle, Joyah French and Marilyn McGuire and Elissa Fesyk, who brought their wisdom and smarts to this project. I so appreciate you all for taking the time to read through this manuscript and share your thoughts with me and with others. Thank you!

*Plouf is the sound a pebble makes when dropped in a river, lake or a pond.

DEDICATED TO

Dr. Arthur Hastings, Ph.D.

Arthur is one of my favorite teachers ever. He taught my first class at the Institute of Transpersonal Psychology, (now Sofia University), entitled *"Introduction to Transpersonal Psychology"*. Arthur brought the transpersonal into the real and tangible world. He made it experience-able, beyond the theoretical and ephemeral language of the mind. He brought it into our hearts and our everyday lives, by modeling principles of open and curious delight in the Universe. He made it all fun by including magic and exercises that allowed us to feel the living, breathing being of the transpersonal world we each are part of.

Arthur was the person that encouraged me to write my dissertation on *"Sailing As A Transformational Experience".* This inevitably led to transformation being the sole focus and foundation of my work as a transformational coach, trainer of the *Transformational Coaching Training Program*, and as a writer. I don't think this would have been possible without the delightful and loving championing that came through Arthur Hastings. This is for you, Arthur.

INTRODUCTION

Transformation is big business these days. It's everywhere. It's in universities and corporations; self-help books, churches and community organizations. But what is it, and how do you know when it has happened to you?

Most people believe that transforming their life will be effortless. Money will suddenly flow, careers will become fulfilling and they will live happily ever after with the sweetheart of their dreams. Truth is; that's the best case scenario. It's the ol' *"For whatsoever a man [woman] soweth, that shall he [she] also reap."*

Transformation isn't all it's cracked up to be. I say this as an expert in the field of transformational coaching and leadership. And I encourage all my clients and trainees to think carefully before embarking on this journey of transforming. It isn't a cake walk and it's definitely not for sissies or the faint of heart.

To transform, one has to cultivate awareness of what they choose to do and think, so they can choose differently – only in service to what they say they want.

One has to change their intentions, their perceptions and orientation, and in many cases change their commitments. It takes a hell of a lot of work, and my experience is that most people just don't want to work that hard. I know I didn't want to work that hard – I still don't. However, I got wrangled into this transformation process as I was backing away from some other life adventure. The title of one of my books, *The Unholy Path of a Reluctant Adventurer*, says it all.

At the same time, I know that each of us has the capacity to be the fullest expression of our unique essential nature. That's why I'm so impassioned with my job as a transformational coach; I continually empower myself to empower you to live into your desire to experience the delight of your full potentiality – whatever that means to you. Both of us transform through the process. That's the fun part that comes after we've done the walking-your-talk stuff; the empowering oneself to move through the messy, raw, vulnerable human stuff; the "What the hell was I thinking?" stuff.

So, I want to give you a few guidelines, signposts, and indicators that will help you along this journey of transformation. Perhaps they will inspire you to keep moving forward through your transformational "whirlwinds," or validate that you really do have the daring necessary to take this journey in the first place. Either way, I think you'll find you are further along the road than you ever imagined.

***My intention for this book was not to be a journal, per se, yet it has, in its unique way, provided a space where journaling can take place. For, you know you are transforming when you can allow what seems to be an inanimate object to inform you of what it wants to be. Enjoy the space in all ways possible.

YOU KNOW YOU ARE
TRANSFORMING WHEN:

YOU KNOW YOU ARE
TRANSFORMING WHEN:

WHAT USED TO
MAKE YOU ANGRY
NOW MAKES YOU SMILE.

#1

YOU KNOW YOU ARE
TRANSFORMING WHEN:

YOU NO LONGER
SPEND TIME & ENERGY COPING
& MANAGING STRESS,
BECAUSE THERE JUST ISN'T ANY.

#2

YOU KNOW YOU ARE
TRANSFORMING WHEN:

YOU NOW EASILY DO THINGS
THAT USED TO SCARE
THE BEEJESUS OUT OF YOU.

#3

YOU KNOW YOU ARE
TRANSFORMING WHEN:

YOU FIND YOURSELF
ABLE TO SIT IN SILENCE
& SIMPLY ENJOY
THE TRANQUILITY OF BEING YOU
& BEING ENOUGH.

#4

YOU KNOW YOU ARE
TRANSFORMING WHEN:

YOU ALLOW YOURSELF
TO FOLLOW YOUR INTUITION
& YOUR HEART,
FOR YOU TRUST YOUR HEART
TO TELL YOU THE TRUTH.

#5

YOU KNOW YOU ARE
TRANSFORMING WHEN:

YOU FIND YOURSELF MORE
PLAYFUL & CREATIVE, DELIGHTING
IN YOUR OWN CREATIONS,
WITHOUT WORRYING
HOW OTHERS MAY JUDGE THEM.

#6

YOU KNOW YOU ARE
TRANSFORMING WHEN:

YOU EFFORTLESSLY
SPEND TIME
DOING WHAT YOU ENJOY,
KNOWING ALL THINGS
ARE IN RIGHT TIMING.

#7

YOU KNOW YOU ARE
TRANSFORMING WHEN:

YOU CHOOSE MORE CAREFULLY
WHICH THOUGHTS
YOU ARE WILLING TO ENTERTAIN,
& WHICH THOUGHTS ARE
NO LONGER WORTH THE BOTHER.

#8

YOU KNOW YOU ARE
TRANSFORMING WHEN:

YOU EXPERIENCE GRATITUDE
FOR THE WAY THINGS ARE
MORE OFTEN THAN YOU
EXPERIENCE RESENTMENT
FOR THE WAY THEY ARE NOT.

#9

YOU KNOW YOU ARE
TRANSFORMING WHEN:

WHEN STRESSED & ANXIOUS,
YOU MORE EFFORTLESSLY
RETURN TO THE PLACE
OF RESTFUL KNOWING,
WHICH YOU'VE CULTIVATED
FOR YOURSELF, BY YOURSELF.

#10

YOU KNOW YOU ARE
TRANSFORMING WHEN:

YOU ACT WHEN YOU
ARE INSPIRED TO DO SO.
YOU KNOW YOU LACK NOTHING
& YOU NEED DO NOTHING
IN THIS MOMENT, EXCEPT
WHAT DELIGHTS & INSPIRES.

#11

YOU KNOW YOU ARE
TRANSFORMING WHEN:

YOU ARE PRESENT
TO THIS MOMENT,
& LESS DISTRACTED
BY WHAT WAS,
WHAT COULD HAVE BEEN,
& WHAT MIGHT BE.

#12

YOU KNOW YOU ARE
TRANSFORMING WHEN:

YOU ACT IN ALIGNMENT
WITH YOUR HIGHEST TRUTH,
BECAUSE YOU KNOW
YOU ARE ALSO ACTING
IN ALIGNMENT WITH
EVERYONE'S HIGHEST TRUTH.

#13

YOU KNOW YOU ARE
TRANSFORMING WHEN:

YOU EXPRESS YOURSELF,
YOUR NEEDS, YOUR WANTS,
YOUR FEELINGS
& YOUR THOUGHTS,
SIMPLY BECAUSE THEY ARE YOURS,
WITHOUT ATTACHMENT
TO OUTCOMES.

#14

YOU KNOW YOU ARE
TRANSFORMING WHEN:

YOU EMPOWER YOURSELF
TO "BE WITH"
WHATEVER CHALLENGES YOU
IN THIS MOMENT,
KNOWING THAT BY DOING SO,
YOU GAIN CAPACITY TO LIVE
IN THE FULLEST POTENTIALITY
OF YOUR BEING.

#15

YOU KNOW YOU ARE
TRANSFORMING WHEN:

YOU WILLINGLY SIT
IN YOUR RESTLESS, IRRITABLE
DISCONTENT, KNOWING
THAT WHAT IS ARISING
IS A CONSEQUENCE
OF EVOLVING SPIRITUALLY,
THROUGH YOUR
HUMAN EXPERIENCE.

#16

YOU KNOW YOU ARE
TRANSFORMING WHEN:

YOU BECOME MORE DISCERNING
ABOUT THE COMPANY YOU KEEP,
BECAUSE YOUR SENSE
OF FULFILLMENT THROUGH
HUMAN CONNECTION
HAS MORE VALUE.

#17

YOU KNOW YOU ARE
TRANSFORMING WHEN:

YOU CHOOSE TO DESIGN
YOUR LIVING SPACE
TO BE MORE IN ALIGNMENT
WITH YOUR REQUIREMENT
FOR RESONANCE
WITH PEACE, LOVE & JOY.

#18

YOU KNOW YOU ARE
TRANSFORMING WHEN:

YOU CHOOSE
TO CHOOSE WHAT YOU CHOOSE
BASED ON
WHAT IS TRUE FOR YOU,
& MUCH LESS ON WHAT
COULD BE SCARY &
MAKES YOU WANT TO PULL AWAY.

#19

YOU KNOW YOU ARE
TRANSFORMING WHEN:

YOU FIND IT MORE EFFORTLESS
TO ENGAGE IN SELF-EXPLORATION
BECAUSE YOU ARE MORE CURIOUS
ABOUT YOURSELF &
HOW YOU HAVE EVOLVED
INTO THIS PRESENT YOU.

#20

YOU KNOW YOU ARE
TRANSFORMING WHEN:

YOU ARE MORE WILLING
TO BE ACCOUNTABLE, NOT
ONLY FOR YOUR MISTAKES,
BUT ALSO FOR YOUR SUCCESSES.

#21

YOU KNOW YOU ARE
TRANSFORMING WHEN:

YOU ARE
HUMBLED
IN THE FACE
OF BEAUTY.

#22

YOU KNOW YOU ARE
TRANSFORMING WHEN:

YOU FIND LIFE
IS EASIER
BECAUSE YOU STOPPED
MAKING IT HARD.

#23

YOU KNOW YOU ARE
TRANSFORMING WHEN:

YOU TALK LESS & LISTEN MORE,
FINDING YOURSELF
FASCINATED BY WHAT
OTHER PEOPLE HAVE TO SAY.

#24

YOU KNOW YOU ARE
TRANSFORMING WHEN:

YOUR SENSE OF PRIDE
& RIGHTEOUSNESS
HAS TAKEN A BACKSEAT
TO DEEP CONNECTION,
TRUE COMMUNICATION,
& COLLABORATION.

#25

YOU KNOW YOU ARE
TRANSFORMING WHEN:

YOU WALK
YOUR TALK,
SAYING WHAT
YOU MEAN,
& MEANING
WHAT YOU SAY.

#26

YOU KNOW YOU ARE
TRANSFORMING WHEN:

THINGS COME
EASILY TO YOU,
BECAUSE YOU'VE
STOPPED BEING ATTACHED
TO HAVING THEM.

#27

YOU KNOW YOU ARE
TRANSFORMING WHEN:

YOU FIND YOURSELF
SMILING
FOR NO REASON AT ALL.

#28

YOU KNOW YOU ARE
TRANSFORMING WHEN:

RANDOM ACTS
OF KINDNESS
BEGIN TO OCCUR
EFFORTLESSLY.

#29

YOU KNOW YOU ARE
TRANSFORMING WHEN:

YOU REALIZE THAT GENEROSITY
DOESN'T REQUIRE YOU
TO GIVE ANYTHING
THAT YOU DO NOT HAVE.

#30

YOU KNOW YOU ARE
TRANSFORMING WHEN:

WHEN GIVING,
YOU EXPERIENCE
A DEEP GRATITUDE
FOR HAVING
SO MUCH.

#31

YOU KNOW YOU ARE
TRANSFORMING WHEN:

YOU DELIGHT
IN OTHER PEOPLE'S SUCCESSES,
LETTING GO
OF YOUR ANGER
THAT IT ISN'T HAPPENING TO YOU.

#32

YOU KNOW YOU ARE
TRANSFORMING WHEN:

YOU SUSPEND
JUDGMENT OF OTHERS,
ACCEPTING THEM AS THEY ARE.

#33

YOU KNOW YOU ARE
TRANSFORMING WHEN:

COMPASSION BECOMES
A MORE FREQUENTED EXPERIENCE,
AS YOU WILLINGLY
ALLOW YOUR HEART
TO OPEN TO ANOTHER'S
HUMAN EXPERIENCE.

#34

YOU KNOW YOU ARE
TRANSFORMING WHEN:

YOU ENJOY
FULFILLING OTHER
PEOPLE'S DESIRES,
JUST BECAUSE.

#35

YOU KNOW YOU ARE
TRANSFORMING WHEN:

YOU FIND THAT
CHOOSING TO SURRENDER
IS COURAGEOUS,
KNOWING YOU ARE IN
ALIGNMENT WITH YOUR
INTEGRITY, RATHER THAN
CAPITULATING OUT OF FEAR.

#36

YOU KNOW YOU ARE
TRANSFORMING WHEN:

THE IDEA OF "SACRIFICE"
DOESN'T ENTER INTO THE
EQUATION ANYMORE.
YOU ARE SIMPLY LETTING GO
OF WHAT NO LONGER SERVES YOU,
YOUR HIGHEST KNOWING
OR YOUR HIGHEST
CONTRIBUTION IN THE WORLD.

#37

YOU KNOW YOU ARE
TRANSFORMING WHEN:

FEAR RARELY INFLUENCES
YOUR CHOICE-MAKING.
YOU KNOW THAT
FEAR IS ACTUALLY
A PART OF ARCHAIC
MEMORY PATTERNS
THAT ARE NOW OBSOLETE &
HAVE NO POWER OVER YOU.

#38

YOU KNOW YOU ARE
TRANSFORMING WHEN:

SELF-RECOGNITION HAS GROWN
INTO SELF-RESPECT,
& HIGHER DEGREES
OF SELF-HONORING.
SOMETIMES YOU DELIGHT
IN MOMENTS OF SELF-LOVE.

#39

YOU KNOW YOU ARE
TRANSFORMING WHEN:

YOU FIND THAT LEVELS
OF CONTENTMENT & HAPPINESS
ARE MORE SUSTAINABLE,
FOR MOMENT BY MOMENT,
YOU ARE GROWING
A SPACE WORTHY OF YOUR
FULLEST EXPRESSION.

#40

YOU KNOW YOU ARE
TRANSFORMING WHEN:

YOUR CHOICE-MAKING
PROCESS RARELY CONCERNS ITSELF
WITH WHAT YOU WILL GAIN.
YOU KNOW THAT
RECEIVING THE ABUNDANCE
THAT IS YOUR BIRTHRIGHT
HAS NOTHING TO DO
WITH WHAT YOU DO.

#41

YOU KNOW YOU ARE
TRANSFORMING WHEN:

YOU FIND THAT YOU ARE
HAVING FUN WHILE WORKING
& WHILE PLAYING.
YOU ARE LOVING WHAT YOU DO,
NO MATTER WHAT.

#42

YOU KNOW YOU ARE
TRANSFORMING WHEN:

SAFETY & SECURITY
ARE NO LONGER
YOUR HIGHEST PRIORITIES,
FOR YOU KNOW YOU ARE
ALWAYS SAFE & SECURE
AS THE ETERNAL PRESENCE
OF DIVINE GRACE.

#43

YOU KNOW YOU ARE
TRANSFORMING WHEN:

BEING FULLY ENGAGED
& PRESENT WITH
THE PEOPLE YOU LOVE
BECOMES YOUR HIGHEST PRIORITY.

#44

YOU KNOW YOU ARE
TRANSFORMING WHEN:

YOU LIE AWAKE AT NIGHT
& ENJOY THE SOLITUDE OF
YOUR OWN COMPANY,
FOR YOU TRUST THAT YOU WILL
HAVE ALL THE REST YOU NEED
TO FACE THE DAY TO COME.

#45

YOU KNOW YOU ARE
TRANSFORMING WHEN:

YOU APOLOGIZE LESS,
FOR THE THINGS YOU DO & SAY,
BECAUSE YOU ARE ACTING
MORE OFTEN IN ALIGNMENT
WITH YOUR OWN INTEGRITY.

#46

YOU KNOW YOU ARE
TRANSFORMING WHEN:

YOU LOVE
WHAT YOU DO
& DO
WHAT YOU LOVE.

#47

YOU KNOW YOU ARE
TRANSFORMING WHEN:

ILLNESS & DIS-EASE
DON'T SCARE YOU SO MUCH,
FOR YOU SEE THEM
AS OPPORTUNITIES
TO FIND OUT THINGS
YOU HAVE YET TO DISCOVER
ABOUT YOURSELF & LIFE, THROUGH
UNPLEASANT CIRCUMSTANCES.

#48

YOU KNOW YOU ARE
TRANSFORMING WHEN:

YOU COMPLETE YOUR TASKS
AT WORK AS IF THEY MATTER,
KNOWING THAT IT'S HOW
YOU "BE" WHILE FULFILLING
MUNDANE WORK
THAT BRINGS A SENSE
OF PEACE & FULFILLMENT
TO YOUR HEART.

#49

YOU KNOW YOU ARE
TRANSFORMING WHEN:

YOU LET GO OF THE NEED
TO WIN RECOGNITION & AWARDS,
FOR YOU KNOW THAT
WHO YOU ARE IS LARGER THAN
THE POWER & THE STATUS THAT IS
GAINED IN THE MUNDANE WORLD.

#50

YOU KNOW YOU ARE
TRANSFORMING WHEN:

THE MONEY IN YOUR POCKET
IS NO LONGER AN
INDICATOR OF YOUR VALUE
& WORTH IN THE WORLD,
FOR YOU KNOW THAT
YOUR WORK IN THE WORLD
HAS NO PRICE TAG ON IT.

#51

YOU KNOW YOU ARE
TRANSFORMING WHEN:

YOU ACCEPT THE CURRENT
CIRCUMSTANCES AS THEY ARE,
FOR YOU KNOW YOU ARE HERE
TO EVOLVE CONSCIOUSNESS
AS A SPIRITUAL BEING.

#52

YOU KNOW YOU ARE
TRANSFORMING WHEN:

YOU WELCOME THE DISCOMFORT
OF THE RELEASE OF CELLULAR &
VIBRATIONAL DENSITY/MEMORIES.
YOU KNOW THIS IS THE ONLY WAY
TO LIGHTEN THE LOAD
OF UNNECESSARY BURDENS –
MOST OF WHICH ARE
UNCONSCIOUS TO YOU.

#53

YOU KNOW YOU ARE
TRANSFORMING WHEN:

YOU VENTURE OUTDOORS
IN ALL KINDS OF WEATHER,
EVEN IN THE RAIN,
SLEET, HAIL & SNOW
KNOWING HOW REFRESHED
& VITAL YOU FEEL
HAVING DONE SO.

#54

YOU KNOW YOU ARE
TRANSFORMING WHEN:

YOU GIVE UP YOUR JOB,
THE MONEY & STATUS NOW,
RATHER THAN
REGRETTING A LIFE OF
TOO MANY HOURS
WITH TOO LITTLE PERSONAL
OR PROFESSIONAL FULFILLMENT.

#55

YOU KNOW YOU ARE
TRANSFORMING WHEN:

YOU WILLINGLY
RELEASE YOUR RESISTANCE
& OPEN TO THE FULL
EXPERIENCE OF GRIEF,
FOR YOU REALIZE IT IS
IMPERATIVE TO RELEASE
WHAT NO LONGER SERVES
OR WHAT WAS NEVER YOURS.

#56

YOU KNOW YOU ARE
TRANSFORMING WHEN:

YOU INTENTIONALLY EXPLORE
THE QUALITIES OF HUMANNESS
SEEN AS "FORBIDDEN",
FOR YOU KNOW
THAT BY BRINGING TO LIGHT
WHAT YOU HAVE HIDDEN,
YOU ALLOW THE UNFOLDING
OF THE FULLEST POTENTIAL
OF YOUR BEING.

#57

YOU KNOW YOU ARE
TRANSFORMING WHEN:

YOU ALLOW YOURSELF
TO EXPERIENCE
POWERLESSNESS THAT COMES
WITH ACKNOWLEDGING
THAT YOU ARE INADEQUATE,
ONLY BECAUSE YOU ARE LIMITED
WITHIN YOUR HUMAN FORM.

#58

YOU KNOW YOU ARE
TRANSFORMING WHEN:

YOU NO LONGER EQUATE
YOUR WORTHINESS WITH
WHAT YOU DO, WHAT YOU MAKE,
WHO YOU ASSOCIATE WITH
OR YOUR SUCCESSES & FAILURES,
FOR YOU KNOW THAT
YOU ARE THE ETERNAL PRESENCE
OF DIVINE GRACE.

#59

YOU KNOW YOU ARE
TRANSFORMING WHEN:

YOU CAN ENTERTAIN
THE QUESTION
"IS LIFE WORTH LIVING?"
WITHOUT THINKING
THAT THERE IS SOMETHING
WRONG WITH YOU,
FOR YOU KNOW THAT
TO ALLOW THE QUESTION
IS PART & PARCEL TO
EXISTING IN HUMAN FORM.

#60

YOU KNOW YOU ARE
TRANSFORMING WHEN:

YOU CONVERSE MORE FREQUENTLY
WITH UNSEEN GUIDES & ANGELS,
KNOWING THAT FEW OF US
HAVE ACCESS TO THE WISDOM
ONLY AVAILABLE IN
THE UNIVERSAL CONSCIOUSNESS.

#61

YOU KNOW YOU ARE
TRANSFORMING WHEN:

YOUR PRAYERS ARE NOT
FOR SEEKING OR HAVING,
FOR YOU KNOW THAT
YOU ALREADY HAVE EVERYTHING,
YOU NEED NOTHING,
& EVERYTHING IS IN
DIVINE HARMONY.

#62

YOU KNOW YOU ARE
TRANSFORMING WHEN:

SURRENDERING YOUR WILL
TO GOD'S WILL
BEGINS TO MAKE A GREAT DEAL
OF SENSE, FOR YOU COME
TO KNOW YOURSELF AS THE DIVINE
SPARK OF ETERNAL
& EVERLASTING LOVE.

#63

YOU KNOW YOU ARE
TRANSFORMING WHEN:

YOU RELY LESS ON HOPE,
FOR YOU KNOW THAT IN THE
STATE OF UNIVERSAL ONENESS
& ENLIGHTENMENT,
HOPE IS AN UNNECESSARY
CONCEPT, & EVERYTHING
IS IN DIVINE PERFECTION.

#64

YOU KNOW YOU ARE
TRANSFORMING WHEN:

YOU NOTICE
PLANTS & FLOWERS,
BUGS & BIRDS,
DREW DROPS & MISTY,
MOISTY MORNINGS.

#65

YOU KNOW YOU ARE
TRANSFORMING WHEN:

YOU WANT TO NURTURE
A LIVING BEING – A PLANT,
AN ANIMAL, A CHILD,
A CREATION OF SOME SORT,
FOR YOU FIND YOURSELF
NURTURED & NOURISHED
IN DOING SO.

#66

YOU KNOW YOU ARE
TRANSFORMING WHEN:

WHAT USED TO BE
A BURDEN, YOU NOW
EXPERIENCE AS A GIFT,
FOR YOU SEE YOUR TRUEST SELF
THROUGH THE ACT
OF CARRYING & CARING.

#67

YOU KNOW YOU ARE
TRANSFORMING WHEN:

IN THE MIDST OF EMOTIONAL
BREAKDOWN, YOU EXPERIENCE
A DEPTH & RICHNESS
THAT CAN ONLY BE REALIZED
BECAUSE YOU ARE HUMAN.

#68

YOU KNOW YOU ARE
TRANSFORMING WHEN:

YOU GIVE AWAY EXPENSIVE
& PRIZED POSSESSIONS,
FOR YOU DELIGHT IN
THE THOUGHT THAT
SOMEONE ELSE WILL ENJOY
THEIR NEW-FOUND TREASURES.

#69

YOU KNOW YOU ARE
TRANSFORMING WHEN:

YOU ARE LIVING IN A
MUCH SMALLER SPACE
WITH SIGNIFICANTLY LESS
MATERIAL BLING-BLINGS
& DO-DADS, YET YOU FEEL
WEALTHIER THAN YOU EVER
THOUGHT POSSIBLE.

#70

YOU KNOW YOU ARE
TRANSFORMING WHEN:

LETTING GO OF CERTAIN
LIFE-LONG FRIENDSHIPS
BRINGS ABOUT A
LIGHTNESS OF BEING,
BECAUSE FOR TOO LONG,
YOU HAVE REMAINED STAGNANT
FOR THE SAKE OF RELATIONSHIPS
THAT DIDN'T GROW YOU.

#71

YOU KNOW YOU ARE
TRANSFORMING WHEN:

IT NOW MAKES SENSE TO YOU
THAT EVEN THE HOMELESS
CAN HAVE GRATITUDE
FOR WHAT THEY HAVE
& WHAT THEY DON'T HAVE.

#72

YOU KNOW YOU ARE
TRANSFORMING WHEN:

YOU INCREMENTALLY RISK
BEING VULNERABLE FOR
THE SAKE OF EXPLORING
THE EDGE OF YOUR WORLD,
FOR OTHERS HAVE DONE SO
& SURVIVED & YOU'RE CURIOUS
TO KNOW IF YOU'LL SURVIVE TOO.

#73

YOU KNOW YOU ARE
TRANSFORMING WHEN:

YOU BEGIN TO QUESTION
GOD AS "THE ALMIGHTY"
– A SINGLE FOCUS
OF POWER & POTENTIAL,
FOR YOU HAVE TOUCHED
GOD AS UNIVERSAL
CONSCIOUSNESS, & KNOW
THE PRESENCE OF DIVINITY
IS EMBODIED WITHIN EVERY
PINPOINT OF EXISTENCE.

#74

YOU KNOW YOU ARE
TRANSFORMING WHEN:

YOU NOTICE SIGNS & SYMBOLS
THAT YOU NEVER NOTICED BEFORE
– INDICATORS THAT
YOU ARE ON THE RIGHT PATH
TO SELF-REALIZATION &
SELF-ACTUALIZATION; ESPECIALLY
WHEN YOU FEEL LOST & ALONE.

#75

YOU KNOW YOU ARE
TRANSFORMING WHEN:

GIFTS APPEAR OUT OF NOWHERE
& RATHER THAN THINKING
YOU'VE "ARRIVED",
YOU REALIZE THAT THESE
ARE SIMPLY INDICATORS
OF YOUR GENERATING
VIBRATIONAL RESONANCE
IN HARMONY
WITH WHAT YOU DESIRE.

#76

YOU KNOW YOU ARE
TRANSFORMING WHEN:

YOU REALIZE IT TAKES
TIME & PRACTICE TO SUSTAIN
THE VIBRATIONAL RESONANCE
THAT CREATES A
HAPPIER-EVER-AFTER REALITY.
FOR BUILDING SUSTAINABILITY,
ONE EXPERIENCE AT A TIME,
IS THE BEST ANY OF US CAN DO.

#77

YOU KNOW YOU ARE
TRANSFORMING WHEN:

YOU INDULGE YOURSELF
IN SMALL LUXURIATING MOMENTS
AS A WAY TO SELF-APPRECIATE
& HONOR YOURSELF.

#78

YOU KNOW YOU ARE
TRANSFORMING WHEN:

YOU NO LONGER RELY
ON SUBSTANCES, ACTIVITY
OR OTHER PEOPLE FOR SERENITY
& ENJOYMENT, FOR YOU SEE
HOW YOU USED THEM TO AVOID,
DISTRACT & DENY A RESTLESS,
IRRITABLE DISCONTENT
THAT YOU SIMPLY COULDN'T
BE WITH ANY OTHER WAY.

#79

YOU KNOW YOU ARE
TRANSFORMING WHEN:

YOU EXPOSE YOURSELF LESS & LESS
TO MEDIA COVERAGE
OF NEGATIVE EVENTS
IN THE WORLD,
FOR YOU KNOW THAT
THESE STORIES
DON'T CONTRIBUTE TO
YOUR HIGHEST TRUTH
OR YOUR HIGHEST GOOD.

#80

YOU KNOW YOU ARE
TRANSFORMING WHEN:

YOU ARE MORE MINDFUL
OF HOW YOU SPEND YOUR TIME,
FOR YOU REALIZE
THE PRECIOUSNESS
OF EVERY MOMENT
OF EVERY DAY.

#81

YOU KNOW YOU ARE
TRANSFORMING WHEN:

YOU BEGIN TO KNOW
THE BIGGER YOU –
THE YOU OF MANY LIFETIMES;
THE YOU THAT IS THE
END RESULT OF A LINEAGE;
THE SPIRITUAL BEING HAVING
A HUMAN EXPERIENCE;
THE YOU THAT IS
UNIVERSAL CONSCIOUSNESS,
ONENESS, SOURCE OF ALL THAT IS.

#82

YOU KNOW YOU ARE
TRANSFORMING WHEN:

YOU QUESTION
YOUR BELIEFS, YOUR JUDGMENTS
& YOUR INTERPRETATIONS
& THEIR ORIGINS,
FOR YOU KNOW THAT
THEY ARE THE CONSEQUENCES
OF LIFETIMES OF EXPERIENCES –
YOURS & OTHERS'.
YOU REALIZE THAT YOU CAN
CHOOSE DIFFERENTLY NOW.

#83

YOU KNOW YOU ARE
TRANSFORMING WHEN:

YOU RECOGNIZE
THE PRECIOUSNESS OF ALL LIFE,
EVEN THAT OF A MOSQUITO,
FOR YOU ARE CULTIVATING
AN AWARENESS & BELIEF
THAT ALL LIFE IS SACRED.

#84

YOU KNOW YOU ARE
TRANSFORMING WHEN:

YOU FIND YOURSELF
LESS IN A RUSH, FOR YOU HAVE
A GREATER CAPACITY
TO EXPERIENCE WHAT IS,
NOW, RATHER THAN BELIEVING
THE GOOD STUFF HAPPENS
ONCE YOU "ARRIVE".

#85

YOU KNOW YOU ARE
TRANSFORMING WHEN:

YOU HAVE A MUCH GREATER
CAPACITY TO BE HERE, NOW,
FOR YOU SEE HOW SENSELESS
IT IS TO LIVE IN THE PAST
OR LIVE INTO THE FUTURE
−NEITHER OF WHICH
TRULY EXISTS.

#86

YOU KNOW YOU ARE
TRANSFORMING WHEN:

THE FOOD YOU
BRING TO YOU,
WHETHER HOME COOKED
OR OTHER, TASTES BETTER,
BECAUSE YOU BRING
MORE LOVE & INTENTION
TO ITS MANIFESTATION.

#87

YOU KNOW YOU ARE
TRANSFORMING WHEN:

YOU PAY YOUR BILLS,
TAXES, & DEBTS ON TIME,
FOR YOU ARE GRATEFUL
FOR ALL THE SERVICES
& OPPORTUNITIES
THAT COME TO YOU.

#88

YOU KNOW YOU ARE
TRANSFORMING WHEN:

ALL THE MIRACLES
THAT HAVE TAKEN PLACE
BROUGHT YOU YOUR REALITY
- JUST THE WAY IT IS.

#89

YOU KNOW YOU ARE
TRANSFORMING WHEN:

YOU HAVE A GREATER CAPACITY
TO PUSH ASIDE NEGATIVE
THOUGHTS, FEELINGS, & STORIES,
BECAUSE YOU'VE CULTIVATED
YOUR CAPACITY TO DO SO.

#90

YOU KNOW YOU ARE
TRANSFORMING WHEN:

YOU ASK FOR ASSISTANCE
& COURAGE TO
"BE WITH" CHALLENGES,
RATHER THAN ASKING
FOR CHALLENGES TO BE REMOVED,
FOR YOU KNOW YOU CAN ONLY
REALIZE WHO YOU TRULY ARE
BY BEING IN DIRECT EXPERIENCE
WITH WHAT'S SCARY &
UNCOMFORTABLE.

#91

YOU KNOW YOU ARE
TRANSFORMING WHEN:

YOU NO LONGER LOOK
FOR THE "MAGIC PILL" OR "BULLET"
THAT WILL TRANSFORM
YOUR LIFE, FOR YOU KNOW
THAT ONLY THROUGH
SELF-EMPOWERED,
SELF-GENERATED ACTIVITY
WILL YOU REALIZE THE
FULFILLMENT OF YOUR DREAMS.

#92

YOU KNOW YOU ARE
TRANSFORMING WHEN:

YOU NOTICE YOU ARE
MAKING CHOICES
YOU COULDN'T HAVE MADE
FIVE MONTHS AGO
& YOU DELIGHT IN
ACKNOWLEDGING
YOUR PROGRESS.

#93

YOU KNOW YOU ARE
TRANSFORMING WHEN:

YOU FOLLOW THROUGH
ON YOUR PROMISES
BECAUSE WHEN YOU DO,
IT FEELS GOOD INSIDE.

#94

YOU KNOW YOU ARE
TRANSFORMING WHEN:

YOU COMMUNICATE CLEARLY
YOUR NEED TO
CHANGE YOUR MIND
OR BREAK AN AGREEMENT,
KNOWING THAT ACTING
IN YOUR HIGHEST GOOD
IS ACTING IN
EVERYONE'S HIGHEST GOOD.

#95

YOU KNOW YOU ARE
TRANSFORMING WHEN:

YOU SIDESTEP THE VOICE
IN YOUR HEAD THAT SAYS,
"WHY SHOULD YOU?
THEY WOULDN'T
DO THAT FOR YOU"
& YOU DO IT ANYWAY,
FOR YOU KNOW IT ISN'T
ABOUT "SHOULD OR SHOULDN'T";
IT'S ABOUT DOING WHAT
YOU BELIEVE NEEDS TO BE DONE.

#96

YOU KNOW YOU ARE
TRANSFORMING WHEN:

YOU WORRY LESS
ABOUT WHAT PEOPLE ARE
GOING TO THINK OR SAY,
FOR YOU'VE COME
TO RESPECT YOUR TRUTH
ABOVE ALL ELSE.

#97

YOU KNOW YOU ARE
TRANSFORMING WHEN:

YOU LAUGH AT YOURSELF MORE
& THOROUGHLY ENJOY
THE WONDER OF YOU
BEING IN EXISTENCE.

#98

YOU KNOW YOU ARE
TRANSFORMING WHEN:

YOU STOP SUCCEEDING
AT FAILING TO BE GREAT,
FOR YOU CAN NO LONGER
HIDE YOUR COMPETENCE
& ABILITY TO FULFILL
ANY DESIRE YOU HAVE –
EVEN TO LOOK LIKE A
PATHETIC, INCOMPETENT FAILURE.

#99

YOU KNOW YOU ARE
TRANSFORMING WHEN:

DEATH-DEFYING LEAPS OF FAITH
ARE EVERYDAY OCCURRENCES,
FOR YOU HAVE CULTIVATED
ENOUGH EXPERIENCE, MAKING
INCREMENTAL CHANGES,
THAT YOU REALIZE THESE SMALL
CHANGES MAKE UP WHAT APPEARS
TO BE A HUGE LEAP!

#100

YOU KNOW YOU ARE
TRANSFORMING WHEN:

NO MATTER WHERE YOU ARE
OR WHAT YOU'RE DOING,
YOU CAN HONESTLY SAY
"IT DOESN'T GET ANY
BETTER THAN THIS".

#101

ABOUT THE AUTHOR

Dr. Rosie Kuhn is an international life and business coach, trainer and speaker. She resides on Orcas Island in the San Juans with her sweet dog, Gracie. Contact Rosie via her website for coaching, training and/or speaking engagements.

www.theparadigmshifts.com

Are you interested in more products connected to this book and it's contents? Please go to:

www.youknowyouaretransformingwhen.com

MORE BOOKS BY DR. ROSIE KUHN

DILEMMAS OF BEING IN BUSINESS

THE ABCS OF SPIRITUALITY IN BUSINESS

SELF EMPOWERMENT 101

THE UNHOLY PATH OF A RELUCTANT ADVENTURER

Please visit **www.theparadigmshifts.com** for more information and to purchase books.